JUNIOR BIOGRAPHIES

Therese M. Shea

ALEXANDER HAMILTON

FOUNDING FATHER AND TREASURY SECRETARY

Enslow Publishing
101 W. 23rd Street
Suite 240
New York, NY 10011
USA
enslow.com

Words to Know

clerk A person who sells goods at a store.

colony A newly settled area that still has ties to the ruling country.

constitution A set of beliefs and laws that determine the role of a country's government and give certain rights to its people.

debt An amount of money owed.

duel A fight between two people that includes the use of weapons.

federal government The central government of a country.

mission A task with a military goal.

sue To try to get a court of law to force a person who has treated you unfairly to give you something or to do something.

tax Money that is paid to the government to cover public costs.

Contents

Alexander Hamilton

CHAPTER 1
YOUNG FOUNDING FATHER

Alexander Hamilton is a name that all Americans know. His face is on the ten-dollar bill. Some people might wonder: How did a man who was not president become so famous? Even though he was young when the nation was forming, Alexander helped shape the country's future.

Alexander Hamilton was born on the island of Nevis in the Caribbean Sea, probably on January 11, 1755. His father, James Hamilton, was a Scottish trader, and his mother, Rachel Fawcett Lavien, was the daughter of a French doctor.

At the time of Alexander's birth, his mother was not married to his father. She had been married to another man who mistreated her, so she ran away to the island of Saint Kitts.

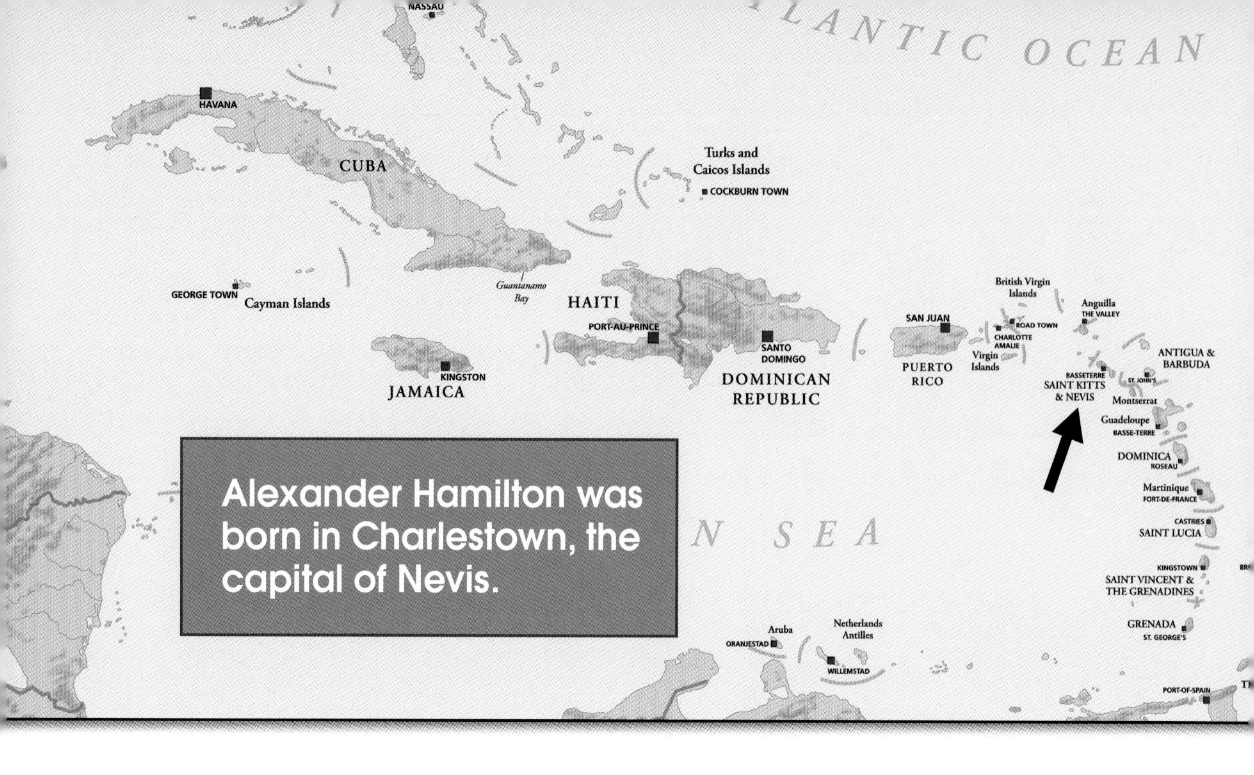

Alexander Hamilton was born in Charlestown, the capital of Nevis.

Growing Up

In 1765, when Alexander was about ten years old, his father left the family. Rachel raised Alexander and his older brother, James, on the island of St. Croix. She set up a shop, and Alexander soon began to work as a clerk. He learned about money and trade. Sadly, Rachel died in 1768, so her family took care of Alexander.

OFF TO AMERICA

Alexander continued to work. His boss saw that he was very smart. He wanted him to have a good education, so he raised money to send Alexander to school in New Jersey. After that, he went to King's College (now Columbia University) in New York City.

It was an exciting time to be living in the colonies. The Americans were unhappy with British taxes. Alexander thought the colonists were right to be upset. When the American Revolution started in 1775, he was ready to fight.

Alexander Says:

"Americans have not, by any acts of theirs, empowered the British Parliament to make laws for them, it follows [Parliament] can have no just authority to do it."

Chapter 2
Soldier and Lawyer

In 1776, Hamilton became a captain in the New York army. At the Battle of Trenton, he and his men stopped the British from attacking George Washington's army. People saw Hamilton's bravery, and he soon met General Washington.

Washington was impressed with the young man and asked him to be his assistant, or aide-de-camp. Hamilton wrote letters for Washington and went on missions. And since Hamilton spoke French, he helped the American and French armies work together.

Shaping the Government

After working for Washington for several years, Hamilton wanted to return to the battlefield. Washington would not allow it at first. The two men argued. Hamilton left his

Hamilton was a captain in the New York army in 1776.

In 1780, during the war, Hamilton married Elizabeth Schuyler, the daughter of an American general from a wealthy New York family.

position and then the military at the end of 1781.

Hamilton moved to Albany, New York, to study law. In 1782, he was elected to represent New York in the Continental Congress, which was now the ruling group of the country. Hamilton believed that the new country needed a strong central government. He thought the states used their powers to work against each other and made the country weaker.

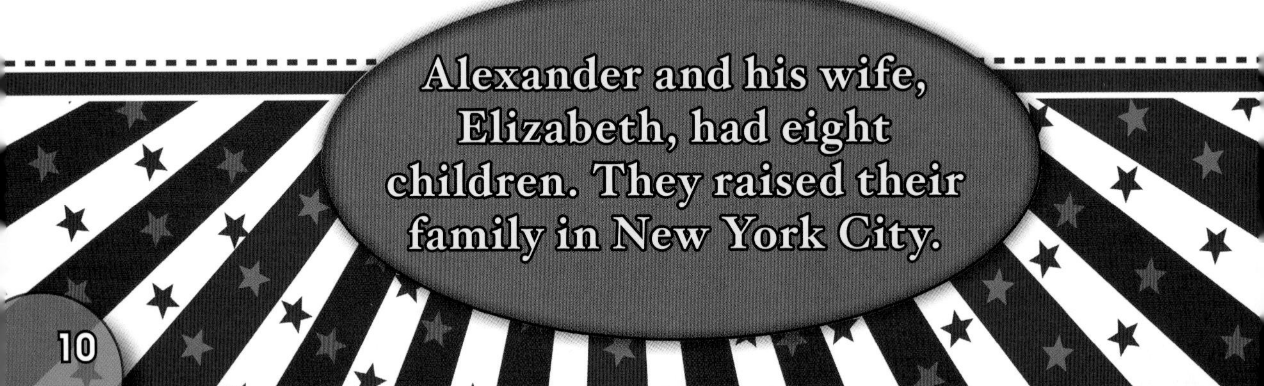

Alexander and his wife, Elizabeth, had eight children. They raised their family in New York City.

Alexander Says:

"Without a shadow of reason and on the slightest ground, [Washington] charged me in the most affrontive manner with treating him with disrespect. I answered very decisively—'Sir I am not conscious of it but since you have thought it necessary to tell me so, we part.'"

Helping the Loyalists

As a lawyer, Hamilton had some tough cases. In one, he had the job of helping British Loyalists who were being **sued**. (Loyalists were American colonists who were on England's side during the revolution.) The Loyalists had taken over property left by colonists who fled New York City during the war. Hamilton argued that the Loyalists

General Washington allowed Hamilton to take part in the Battle of Yorktown in 1781, the last major battle of the American Revolution. Here, the British surrender after the battle.

did not have to pay for using the property because of agreements made in the peace treaty at the end of the war. Hamilton won his case. It was an important decision that is still used in courts today.

Chapter 3
Creating a Constitution

In May 1787, people from all thirteen states met to talk about the country's problems. The meeting was in Philadelphia, Pennsylvania, and was called the Constitutional Convention. Hamilton represented New York.

Hamilton argued for replacing the existing constitution, called the Articles of Confederation, with a new constitution. He wanted to make the federal

Alexander Says:

"The system [in the Constitution], though it may not be perfect in every part, is, upon the whole, a good one; is the best that the present views and circumstances of the country will permit; and is such an one as promises every species of security which a reasonable people can desire."

The Constitutional Convention meets in 1787. Alexander Hamilton is slightly left of center of the picture, seated, speaking to Benjamin Franklin, also seated, holding a cane.

government stronger, but also give some powers to the states.

Along with James Madison and John Jay, Hamilton tried to persuade the states to approve the US

Constitution. They wrote eighty-five essays now called *The Federalist Papers.* The US Constitution was finally approved in 1788.

George Washington meets with members of his first cabinet, Thomas Jefferson (*left*) and Hamilton (*center*).

Handling the Nation's Money

In 1789, George Washington was elected president of the United States. He made Alexander Hamilton secretary of the treasury. This was not an easy job. At that time, the country was in debt because of the American Revolution. Hamilton had

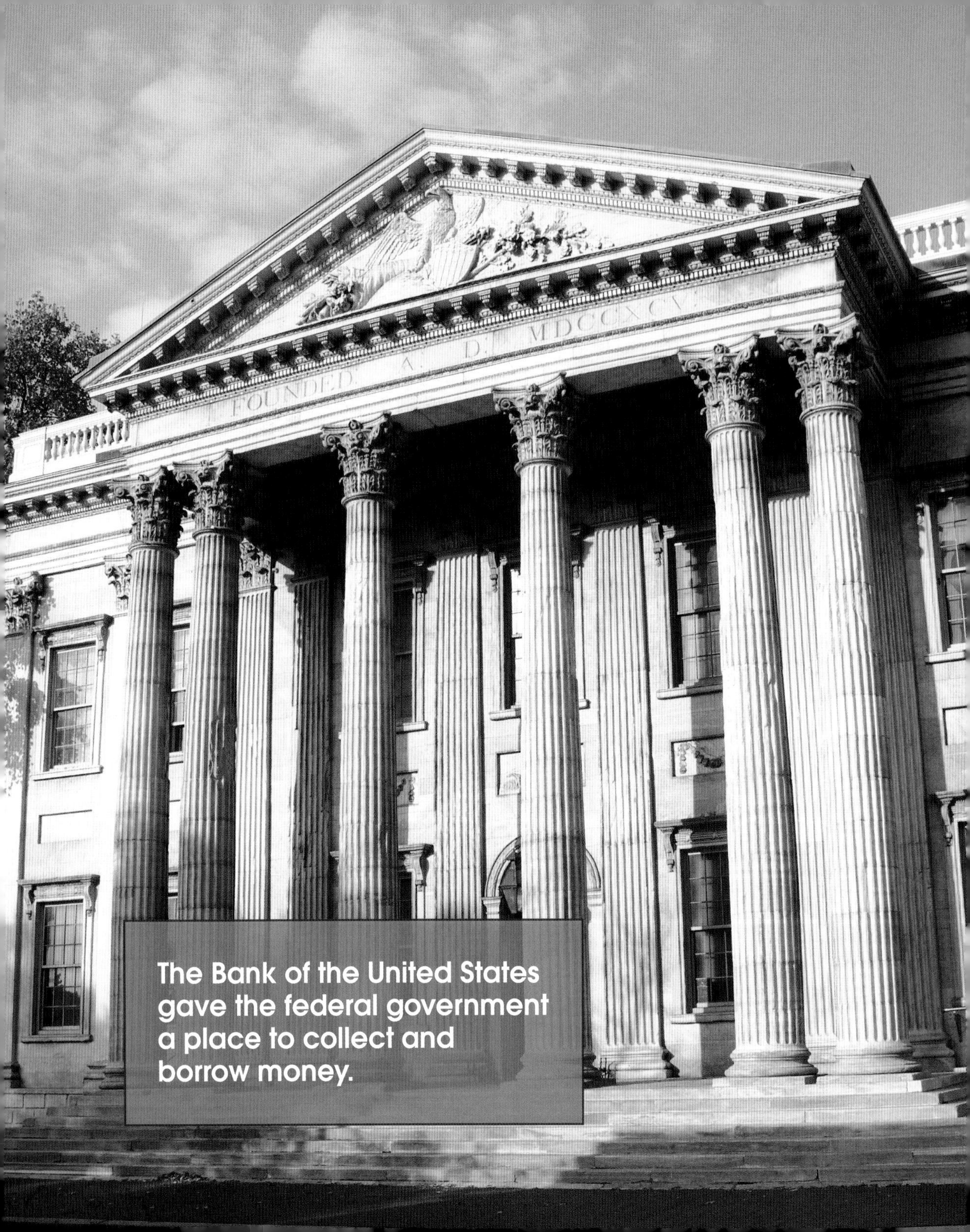

The Bank of the United States gave the federal government a place to collect and borrow money.

a plan. The federal government would pay the states' debt, and the American people would pay back the money in taxes.

Hamilton also started the Bank of the United States. He wanted this bank to be in charge of money for the whole country. Many people disliked this idea and thought it gave too much power to the federal government. Still, it was signed into law.

Hamilton got support for his ideas about debt and taxes by making an agreement with James Madison. Madison promised that the government would support Hamilton if the nation's capital were placed along the Potomac River. That area became Washington, DC.

Chapter 4
Enemies in Government

Hamilton worked hard to make the government better, but many people did not like his ideas. New political parties were formed. The people who wanted a strong federal government, like Hamilton, were called Federalists. Those who supported more states' rights were called Republicans.

The Duel

Hamilton often made enemies because of his strong views. One of these was Aaron Burr. In 1804, Hamilton worked against Burr, who was running to become governor of New York. Burr lost the election and was angry at Hamilton, who once called him "the most unfit and dangerous man of

Alexander Says:

"The honor of a nation is its life."

This artwork shows the duel between Hamilton and Burr, who was vice president of the United States at the time. Honor duels were illegal in most states.

the community." Burr challenged Hamilton to a duel. Hamilton accepted.

At dawn on July 11, 1804, Alexander Hamilton and Aaron Burr faced each other in Weehawken, New Jersey. They drew their guns and fired. Hamilton missed. Burr

The award-winning musical *Hamilton* has increased people's interest in Alexander Hamilton's amazing life story.

Hamilton disliked duels. His son Philip died in one in 1801. However, Hamilton believed he had to accept the challenge or he would lose "the ability to be in the future useful."

hit Hamilton. Hamilton was taken back to New York City, where he died the next day.

A Loyal American

Alexander Hamilton left a lasting mark on American history. He made the nation stronger and set up systems that are still in place today. He was loyal to his country, and he worked hard to make sure it would last. He started off as a poor child in the Caribbean and became a powerful man in the government. Hundreds of years later, it is still a remarkable American story.

Timeline

1755 Alexander Hamilton is born on the island of Nevis, probably on January 11.

1772 Moves to New Jersey to study.

1774 Writes "A Full Vindication of the Measures of Congress" while studying in New York.

1775 Joins New York army at start of American Revolution.

1777 Becomes George Washington's aide-de-camp during the American Revolution.

1780 Marries Elizabeth Schuyler.

1787 Represents New York at the Constitutional Convention in Philadelphia. With others, begins writing essays now called *The Federalist Papers.*

1789 Becomes first secretary of the treasury.

1804 Hamilton and Aaron Burr duel in Weehawken, New Jersey, on July 11. Hamilton dies the next day.

Learn More

Books

Brown, Don. *Aaron and Alexander: The Most Famous Duel in American History*. New York, NY: Roaring Brook Press, 2015.

Kelley, K. C. *Alexander Hamilton: American Hero.* New York, NY: Scholastic, 2017.

Kulling, Monica. *Alexander Hamilton: From Orphan to Founding Father.* New York, NY: Random House, 2017.

Websites

The American Experience: Alexander Hamilton

pbs.org/wgbh/amex/duel/peopleevents/pande06.html

Learn more about this Founding Father's life.

History.com: Alexander Hamilton

history.com/topics/american-revolution/alexander-hamilton

Watch a video about Hamilton's life and works.

INDEX

Published in 2018 by Enslow Publishing, LLC.
101 W. 23rd Street, Suite 240, New York, NY 10011

Library of Congress Cataloging-in-Publication Data

Names: Shea, Therese M., author.
Title: Alexander Hamilton : founding father and treasury secretary / Therese M. Shea.
Description: New York, NY : Enslow Publishing, LLC, [2018] | Series: Junior biographies | Includes bibliographical references and index. | Audience: Grades 3-5.
Identifiers: LCCN 2017011022| ISBN 9780766090453 (pbk.) | ISBN 9780766090460 (6 pack) | ISBN 9780766090477 (library bound)
Subjects: LCSH: Hamilton, Alexander, 1757-1804–Juvenile literature. | Statesmen–United States–Biography–Juvenile literature. | United States–Politics and government–1783-1809–Juvenile literature.
Classification: LCC E302.6.H2 S54 2018 | DDC 973.4092 [B] –dc23
LC record available at https://lccn.loc.gov/2017011022

Printed in China

To Our Readers: We have done our best to make sure all website addresses in this book were active and appropriate when we went to press. However, the author and the publisher have no control over and assume no liability for the material available on those websites or on any websites they may link to. Any comments or suggestions can be sent by email to customerservice@enslow.com.

Photo Credits: Cover, p. 1 Stock Montage/Archive Photos/Getty Images; p. 4 DEA Picture Library/De Agostini/Getty Images; p. 6 Peter Hermes Furian/Alamy Stock Photo; p. 9 Interim Archives/Archive Photos/Getty Images; p. 10 Science History Images/Alamy Stock Photo; p. 12 Library of Congress Prints and Photographs Division; p. 14 GraphicaArtis/Archive Photos/Getty Images; p. 15 Three Lions/Hulton Archive/Getty Images; p. 16 Gary Whitton/Shutterstock.com; p. 19 H. Armstrong Roberts/ClassicStock/Archive Photos/Getty Images; p. 20 Theo Wargo/WireImage/Getty Images; back cover, pp. 2, 3, 22, 23, 24 (curves graphic) Alena Kazlouskaya/Shutterstock.com; interior page bottoms (crowd) nalinn/Shutterstock.com.